Life in a Castle

by Althea

Illustrations by Hilary Abrahams

Produced by Dinosaur Publications for
Cambridge University Press

Cambridge
London   New York   New Rochelle
Melbourne   Sydney

About the first people to build castles in Britain were the Normans. The earliest ones were made of wood and they actually brought some of the wooden sections over the sea from Normandy. Castles were built as fortresses to make it as difficult as possible for enemies to attack. First a huge mound of earth called a Motte was made and then the castle was built on top of it. This tower-shaped building was called the Keep. A ditch was dug around the base of the Motte, and when full of water this made a moat which was difficult for enemies to cross. This was then surrounded by a strong wooden fence called a Palisade and yet another ditch was dug outside the palisade. But one way enemies could take a castle was to set fire to the gates and to try to stop this, main entrances started to be built of stone. From 1150 onwards they started to make the whole castle of stone.

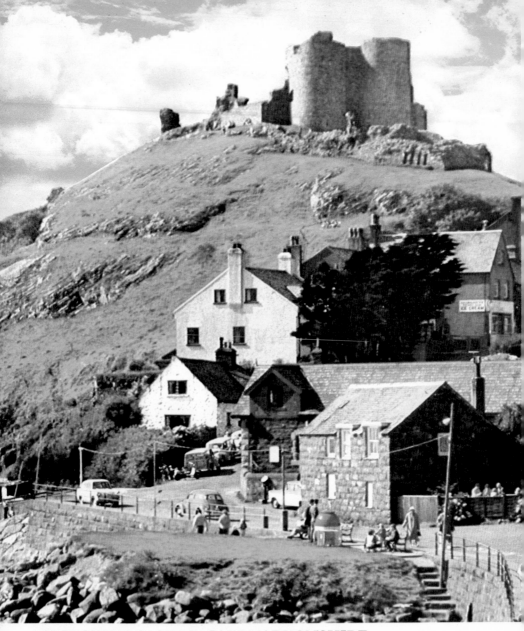

CRICCIETH CASTLE, CAERNARVONSHIRE

The first castle at Criccieth was built in about 1230. When Edward I conquered North Wales he spent a lot of money rebuilding and strengthening castles and Criccieth was one of these. There is a record of a bill for improvements dated 1292 for £306, but this was not a lot of money because new castles like Harlech and Caernarvon had £8,000 spent on them at that time. William de Leyburn was Constable of the Garrison at one time, and in 1284 his pay was £100 a year. The castle included a platform for a machine which threw huge rocks at besieging soldiers.

DOLBADARN CASTLE, CAERNARVONSHIRE

Dolbadarn is another Welsh Castle and was probably built around the end of the 13th Century. It is built on a narrow piece of rock with steep slopes at each side which gives it a very commanding position near the Llanberis Pass. The main tower shows clearly the entrance on the first floor, which made entry by invaders difficult. The floor beneath this could probably only be reached through a trapdoor from the first floor. The main keep included a portcullis, which was an iron lattice gate with spikes on the bottom which could be dropped down if the castle was attacked.

Castles were built by the great Barons who each owned large areas of the country, now called counties. They often quarrelled and fought between themselves, and attacks on castles happened fairly often. The King, when travelling across the country from one place to another, would usually stay in the castles of various Barons and there began to be great rivalry between the barons in owning impressive castles. Some Barons were so rich that they had several castles in different parts of the country. They travelled from one to another, living in each for a few months of the year, when they would check up on their estates and live off the food which had been grown there.

The earliest stone castles were large towers with the entrance high up on the first floor. It was impossible for anyone to arrive unnoticed, because soldiers stood guard on the roof or battlements and could see anyone approaching for miles around.

The tower, or keep, of the castle was usually in a large courtyard, and the wall of this courtyard had smaller towers spaced along it, each with more look-out places.

DOVER CASTLE, KENT

Dover Castle has one of the best examples of a square Norman keep
in Britain. Henry II built it, and the work was completed in 1187.
The keep is nearly 100 feet square and about 90 feet high. All castles
have massive walls against bombardment, and the walls of Dover
Castle keep are 22 feet thick at the base. The main keep is protected by
an inner line of rampart walls and towers and an outer line was later
added during the 13th Century. A lot of the additional work to the
Castle towards the end of the 12th Century was done by a man
called 'Maurice the Engineer.'

BRAEMAR CASTLE, ABERDEENSHIRE
Braemar Castle was built in 1628 by the Earl of Mar. English troops used it as a barracks after the defeat of the Jacobite Rebellion in 1746 and it is now owned by the Farquharson family.

The Baron's soldiers who defended his castle needed protection from enemy weapons, and special clothing was invented for this. Various kinds of armour were used, and as weapons became more dangerous, the clothing had to give more protection. At the Battle of Hastings in 1066, soldiers wore mail tunics and conical metal helmets. The mail tunics were made up of hundreds of metal rings linked together.

At the Armoury in the castle it was the Armourer's job to keep all the weapons in good order. To clean the rust off mail he used to put the tunics into a barrel of sand and vinegar and then get a boy to roll the barrel along. The Armourer also had to keep the shields, swords and helmets polished. After many years, whole suits of plate armour were invented. They were quite heavy but the weight of the suit was spread evenly over the whole body and the special joints made it easy to move about. But armour was very expensive, the best being made in Italy and Germany, so only rich noblemen and knights could afford to have suits of armour.

Some soldiers were professionals and so were paid. They had to supply their own weapons. Guarding the castle was also shared by tenants whom the baron ordered to duty from time to time. These tenants were usually poorly equipped so the castle armourers always kept a good stock of swords, crossbows, and other weapons for their use.

CAWDOR CASTLE, NAIRNSHIRE

Cawdor Castle was built by the Thane of Cawdor after having dreamt that a donkey told him to build his house where he lay down under a hawthorn tree. The castle was used as the scene for Duncan's murder in the play "Macbeth" by Shakespeare.

DUNVEGAN CASTLE, ISLE OF SKYE

The best known castle on Skye is Dunvegan which is the seat of the
Chieftain of the Clan Macleod. Parts of the castle include 13th, 14th
and 15th Century additions.

The head of the castle household was the Baron, but he was often away either on hunting trips, attending the King at Court, or fighting in the Royal Army. His wife was next in charge, and she was always travelling round visiting their different manors.

After the Lord and Lady came the Steward. He acted as a general manager for the Baron, and saw that the other officials carried out their work. There was also a man called the Wardrober or Treasurer. He was in charge of all the stores, because a wardrobe was a place for storing valuable goods, not just somewhere to hang clothes as it is today!

Every castle had a Chaplain or cleric who was responsible for writing the letters as he was one of the few people who could write. The Marshal was in charge of the horses, of which there were a great many, and he also arranged all the travelling when the family household moved to one of their other castles. The Porter looked after the main gate and held the keys to the castle.

The Baron's knights also lived in. So did all the servants and other officials who helped to run the castle. A household of 100 people or so was quite usual.

The most important room in the castle was the Great Hall. This was on the first or second floor of the main tower or Keep. It was used for business, eating and sleeping, and for entertainment. Many of the household slept in it on benches, or wrapped in cloaks lying on rushes on the floor. There was a small room built into the thickness of the wall of the Great Hall called the Treasury and the baron's treasure was stored there. This was a chest containing gold coins, jewellery, silver cups, dishes and candlesticks, and other valuable items. Copies of written agreements with his tenants were stored there too. The Baron also kept his best wine in the Treasury.

Glass was scarce, and they used oiled parchment for the windows. They used to take down the parchment and move it with them when they travelled to another castle.

In another corner of the Hall was the wellhead, with its chain and bucket for drawing water. There was also a doorway leading to the privy-chamber or lavatory. On the same floor, or sometimes upstairs from the Hall, the baron and his wife had their private rooms which were a combined sitting room and bedroom. The bed was curtained off from the rest of the room with drapes around it—later on these became four-poster beds. Quite often, a teenage daughter or ladiesmaid slept in the same room as the baron and his lady in a small bed. On the same floor were other sleeping chambers for knights, household officials and guests to the castle. Then there was a large dormitory for the maidservants and they used this as a sewing room during the day, too. Above this were the battlements and the roof of the Keep. In times of trouble paid soldiers were up on the roof keeping watch, but when it was peaceful it was the tenants' duty to come in and do this.

The kitchen was below the Great Hall, or in a separate building in the courtyard. In the foundations of the castle were the cellars and dungeons, and sometimes prisoners were kept in these.

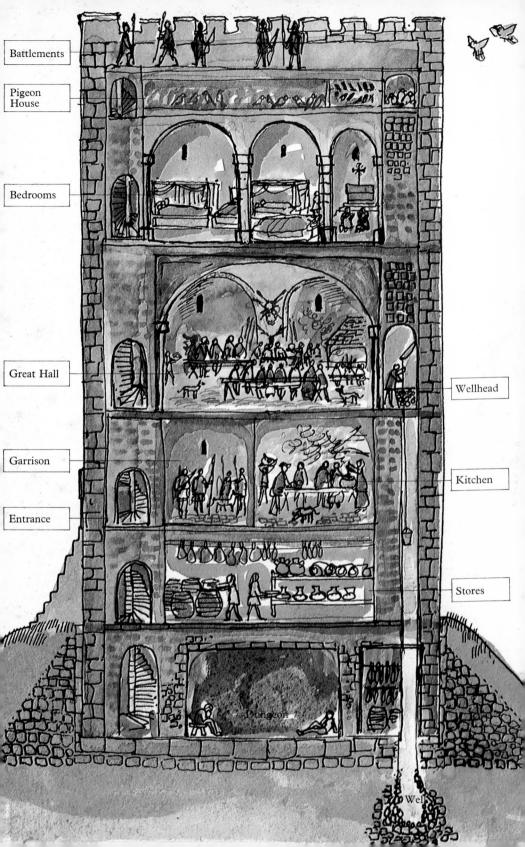

Battlements

Pigeon House

Bedrooms

Great Hall

Garrison

Entrance

Wellhead

Kitchen

Stores

Dungeon

Well

During the day the Steward and the other officials did their business in the Great Hall. The estate was run from the castle and the tenants used to come to it to pay rents for their land, and sort out their problems and squabbles under the guidance of the Baron. All the business of a town or county council which happens from a Town or Shire Hall was the responsibility of the Baron.

At dinner time the long trestle tables were set out. Here everyone assembled for the main meal of the day. The top table had drinking cups and spoons made of silver. The rest of the places were set with earthenware cups and wooden or horn spoons. Everyone washed their hands at wash stands as they entered the hall. A servant would bring a bowl to the top table for the Lord and his guests to wash their hands.

The hall was heated by a large open fire. In some castles there were no chimneys and as the walls got black and smoky they had to be whitewashed fairly often.

At the end of the day the planks and trestles were stacked away again to make room for people to lie down and go to sleep.

The kitchens were large and an important part of life in the castle. Food was cooked in great quantities. Some food, such as cheese and butter was made in the district and brought into the castle, but most of the things were prepared in the kitchens. Sacks of flour would arrive and the baker then sifted and sorted it. The finest flour was used to make white loaves for the Baron's table, and the rest of the household had coarser wholewheat bread. Everyone used a thick slice of day-old bread called a trencher as a plate to eat their food from.

The Baron and the people at the top table usually drank wine, which mostly came from France, probably from the English province of Gascony. But ale was made in the castle from barley and rye and was quite cheap enough to allow everyone some with their dinner.

The meat was much the same as we eat today, beef, mutton, pork, bacon and ham. Chicken and geese were another favourite, and their feathers were used to make feather beds and pillows. Big sides of meat were cooked on a spit over an open fire and some of the kitchen staff had to turn the spit so that the meat cooked evenly all round. They used big iron cauldrons to cook soup and stews in. They ate a lot of fish too, particularly dried herrings.

People got up early in the castle, and had only a hunk of bread before starting their work. The main meal of the day, dinner, was at about 10 or 11 o'clock in the morning.

Many castles had herb gardens. The herbs were grown both to flavour food, and to make medicines and ointments.

They grew saffron and mustard in the garden but most spices were very expensive because they had to be imported from the East by ship. They were kept locked in the wardrobe and the cook had to ask for what he needed. Meat had to be salted and stored for the winter, because there was only enough hay to keep a few animals alive for breeding the next year. So spices were used to disguise the taste of the meat which was sometimes going off a bit. For fresh meat they bred pigeons, which were made into game pie. Salt, which was mainly mined in Cheshire, used to be bought from travelling salt merchants.

Even when no battles were being fought and the baron was at peace with his neighbours, it was still very necessary to keep up the training of his men and his horses. Soldiers had to be trained to use the crossbow or to use a sword. Some of the training was made into a game, and they had tilting competitions with lances and mock battles called tournaments.

Other people in the castle would be busy looking after its upkeep— mending a leaking roof, making new trestle tables, perhaps tending the herb gardens or the orchard. Inside the keep, the sewing ladies were busy making clothes for all the household. These were supplied free, usually at Christmas time as part of wages, and were called livery.

The Baron's sons were given lessons by the Chaplain. As they got older they were usually sent away to another castle as pages to learn the manners and behaviour which was expected of a nobleman.

In the evenings after supper in the Great Hall everyone played games such as chess or draughts. Perhaps someone would get up and sing to entertain them, many of the company joining in. Sometimes travelling minstrels would call at the castle and play their instruments.

Carn Brae Castle, Redruth

Here are some more castles. Of course there are many others. Perhaps you could collect postcards of the ones you have visited.

Rowallan Castle, Kilmarnock

Delgaty Castle, Turrif

Blair Castle, Perthshire

Windsor Castle

Arundel Castle, Sussex

Caernarvon Castle, North Wales

Henry VIII Gateway, Windsor Castle